House Repairs

Other Works from Angela Jackson-Brown

Fiction
Drinking from a Bitter Cup

Plays
Anna's Wings
Black Lives Matter (Too) It Is Well
Wade in the Water

FULL PRAISE FOR *HOUSE REPAIRS*

"I have often said that good poetry makes you think or feel deeply; great poetry makes you do both. And great poetry is not found in lofty ideals like Truth, Nature, God, or Love. It happens where life happens, down in the midst of things, in the spaces between our hearts. Angela Jackson-Brown's *House Repairs*, is great poetry. In it you will find what makes poetry necessary. You will find honesty and pain, beauty and atonement in these poems, where the power of strangled and realized possibility sings. Jackson-Brown is an accomplished teacher, novelist, and playwright, but this, her first poetry collection, shows the world what I have known for decades: She is a great poet. Indeed, her power as a poet is what makes those other avenues of accomplishment possible. Indulge yourself here in these pages. Experience an irrepressible voice; ready for battle, setting long silences free."

– Robert Gray
Author of *Drew: Poems from Blue Water* &
Jesus Walks the Southland

"Angela Jackson-Brown offers herself... no, she **announces** herself to us as Spirit-Woman, and we would do well to heed the histories of hurts and healings woven beautifully and brutally through her poetry. She eviscerates in one three line poem only to coax us back and salve us with long, loving wordstrokes in the next. It has been a long time since I have cried and laughed with such abandon in the pages of a single volume. *House Repairs* strikes me as a gift earned from earth and blood and offered to the reader with grace."

– Colleen S. Harris
Author of *The Kentucky Vein, These Terrible Sacraments*
& *God in My Throat: The Lilith Poems*

"Early on in this debut collection, Angela Jackson-Brown admits she's writing from her own life, but that isn't exactly true. Instead, I would say she's redefined it – redefining what it is to be black, what it is to be a woman with her real woman's body, and most of all, what it is to survive in a world that did not always want her and in which she did not always even want her own self. This is especially poignant considering her story begins in the post-Jim-Crow South of kudzu and muscadine wine where she was made to go to a segregated bathroom when she was only five (and – God help us – it was already

1973). In these self-searching songs of survival, she calls her chosen matriarchy of Alice Walker and Maya Angelou by name, writing her way out and eventually arriving at a life she can fully claim as her own. As she says in her penultimate poem, 'I can finally see the ancestors in me for the first time / and they, likewise, can finally see me, and they, / with smiles of recognition, / acknowledge and welcome me home.' For that alone, her journey is a crowning achievement and a model of strength."

– **Nickole Brown**
Author of *Sister* and *Fannie Says: A Biography-in-Poems*

HOUSE REPAIRS

Angela Jackson-Brown

Negative Capability PRESS

House Repairs
© October 2018, Angela Jackson-Brown

Edited by Andrew Rosser
Cover Design by Megan Cary
Interior Design by Jacob Burkhardt

ISBN 978-0-942544-47-3
Library of Congress Control Number: 2018909220

Negative Capability Press
64 Ridgelawn Drivee East
Mobile, Alabama 36608
(251) 591-2922

Find us online at:
negativecapabilitypress.org
facebook.com/negativecapabilitypress

*Dedicated to the memory of M.C. Jackson,
Judith Brown and Gwendolyn Pendleton.*

ACKNOWLEDGMENTS

The following poems (sometimes in slightly different versions) first appeared in the following magazines, journals and plays:

A Narrow Fellow: Journal of Poetry. "Vacation" and "The Naked Truth"; *Uptown Mosaic Magazine*: "Frigid," Bitch," and "Dry Bones"; *94 Creations*: "Hush" and "I Am Not Your Corporate Mammy"; *The 2009 Limestone Dust Poetry Festival Anthology*: "Country Folk" and "Naked Communion"; *Pet Milk Literary Journal*: "Locs" and "Where the Music At"; *When Women Wakens.* "we cut" and "Yearning for a Savior"; *Identity Theory.* "I Belong to Pan," "Real Talk About Back in the Day," and "Play Me One of Those Old School Joints: And I'll Be Yours Tonight." *Toe Good Poetry.* "Bacchus, Are You There." Excerpts from "Black Girl Magic" and "You Black" appear in the play, *Black Lives Matter (Too).*

EDITOR'S NOTE

Writing saved my life. I don't mean it in some metaphorical way where I wrote down my feelings and put away the dark thoughts in a leather down book. I mean, it quite literally, saved my life. There were times where writing was the only think that could get me through the day. Knowing that taking a pen to the page and bleeding ink over the sawed down tree would make me feel better is what saved my life. For many of us, this is the case. I wrote to save myself from my own past where I thought I would never escape. Angela, however, has written her past and shown us a way to take it and move forward. To take our grief and force it to submit to our own will.

In Angela's poem, *Hush,* she tells us what happens. With so few words, effective use of the white space, and mindful dialogue, we know what the speaker faces in this poem. Silence. A silence so deafening and heart- wrenching there is no other option than to be silent in it's presence... Angela persists through this silence though and shows us what it means to be loud in the strong back of silence.

Through this collection I have cried and loved and to have known Angela as a colleague, mentor, and a friend is a blessing. Having the opportunity to know her more in this collection, I invite you, to read this book and get to know Angela as I have; honestly and intimately.

– Andrew Rosser

INTRODUCTION

I never thought I would write a book about my life. I love reading memoirs and autobiographies about the lives of people I admire, but the idea of telling my own story seemed strange because I never truly felt like there was anything remarkable about my life. I have struggled and I have succeeded, and none of those things seemed inspiring enough to share with others.

But as time went on, I changed my mind. The first autobiography I ever read was Maya Angelou's *I Know Why the Caged Bird Sings*. I was eleven when I read that book and shortly afterwards, I, too, was sexually molested by a family member. The thing that got me through that horrible time in my life was Dr. Angelou's story. Many times during my childhood, I said to myself, "If Miss Angelou could make it through her tragedy, I could too."

I even wrote her a letter to tell her thank you for writing such an inspirational book, but I was such an insecure young girl, I was afraid she would reject me, or worse, not even acknowledge my letter, so, I found my daddy's cigarette lighter, and I went outside and burned the letter I had written to Dr. Angelou, along with some of the other writing I had done that I didn't deem worthy enough to exist in this world anymore. (Yes, I have been fairly dramatic my entire life.) Years later, I got the chance to go and hear Dr. Angelou speak, and even though I was in my thirties, I still felt like an insecure young girl inside, so I didn't even go up to her to say thank you or take a picture. I still didn't feel worthy to be in her presence. So, I simply sat and thought to myself, *that woman has saved my life time and time again through her words, and she doesn't even know it.*

After Dr. Angelou died, I began to question my fear of writing my own memoir. I started saying to myself, *you have a story that others might need to hear so that they, too, can be healed.* Because above all else, I always believed, words have the power to transform lives, starting with my own. As I started to look at my life in those terms, I realized, I have a lot to share. I was adopted. I was shown unconditional love by only one of my adopted parents. I lived through the so-called post-Jim Crow south. I survived mental and physical abuse. I dealt with mental issues, thoughts of suicide, and an overall mistrust of people. I endured a traumatic divorce AND I found love with a man who has spent every day we have been together showing me what love really looks like. All of those things are worth sharing. So, I attempted to write my story in prose form, but I realized that for me, I needed poetry to tell my story right.

Telling my story through poetry gives me a freedom to get close to parts of my life without having to dwell in those moments for extended periods of time. Poetry frees my soul and allows me to distill my emotions into compact literary snapshots. Poetry allows me to access language in ways that I am still attempting in my fiction. So, I finally gave in to the spirits that guide me when I write, and I wrote this collection of poems. My hope is that *House Repairs* helps others as much as it helped me to write it.

I call this collection *House Repairs* because life is a continual process of rebuilding, remodeling and re-envisioning ourselves. Sometimes we are in total disrepair and other times we are firm in the foundation we have created for ourselves through the struggles we have had to endure. My hope is that this book will continue to remind me of how far I have come and will remind others that they too can embark on a journey of renewal and healing, and yes, rebuilding.

TABLE OF CONTENTS

When a Mother Leaves a Child   1
He Went Gentle   2

A House Condemned

The Death of My Pen   5
Roots Unfurled   6
A Midwife's Lament   8
Country Folk   9
History: A Poem About Water Under the Bridge   10
Dark Child   11
Hush   12
Mommy Issues: A Poem of Dismissal   13
Consecrated Blood   14
Memories: A Young Child's Past-Tense   16
Yearning for a Savior   17
These Hips, These Hips, Lord God These Hips   18
Dear Mama   20

A House Demolished

Phantom Baby   23
The Naked Truth   25
Frigid   27
Sorry   28
Bitch   29
Vacation   30
I Must Not Breathe   32
I'm Tired of Living in a World   33

A House Salvaged

Dry Bones   37
Black Girl Magic   38
I Tried to Write You A Love Poem   40
    but Then It Became About Me
Having A Love Affair with My Damn Self   41
Blues High   44

I Am Not Your Corporate Mammy   46

Play Me One of Those Old School Joints   47
     and I'll Be Yours Tonight

Bacchus, Are You There?   48

Naked Communion   51

I Belong to Pan   53

You Black   55

We Cut   57

A House Rebuilt

Karma   61

Rebirth   62

An Ode to My Rebellious Son   63

Spirit Woman   64

Where the Music At?   65

Locs   67

House Repairs   69

WHEN A MOTHER LEAVES HER CHILD

In loving memory of Gwendolyn Pendleton

No matter how old you are, you want her to stay.
Even if your face has been kissed with wrinkles;
even if your hair has thinned or white strands have begun
to outnumber the darker hairs of your youth;
even if you walk a little slower and your back is slightly bent;
even if you, too, are a parent or a grandparent;
you never want your mother to leave.

You never stop wanting your mother's embrace. You never
stop wanting your mother's words of wisdom. You never
stop wanting to hear her tell you she loves you. You never
stop wanting her warm breath against your face. You never
stop wanting to climb into her lap and have her rock you
into a gentle sleep. You never stop wanting your mother.

When your mother finally does go away, that part of your heart that
belonged to her and her alone, crumbles just a little. You think at any
moment you too might leave, that the pain of her absence
might be enough to take you out too, but inside you hear her whisper,
*It's not your time. You must stay and know that even though
I'm gone, I'm not really gone.*

You hear her say to you: *See your eyes, those eyes are
mine looking back at you. See that smile, that is my smile
on your precious face. Listen to that laugh, that's all mine too.
I'm with you, she says, even when I'm not, because you are me,
and I am you.*

Death is merely a bridge that we must cross over,
and although it feels like we are separated from those we love
we aren't, not really, because pieces of those we love will
always dwell inside of us. Parts of them leave, but the parts
that matter, their undying love, it remains as long as we
have memory and breath.

So, mothers never truly leave their children when they die,
because their love lives on for all eternity and beyond.

HE WENT GENTLE
In loving memory of M.C. Jackson

Daddy went to sleep.
That was it.
No grand speeches;
no fond farewells;
no wink of the eye;
no "Hang in there, kid."

I was expecting more.
I had prepared myself for one last
something.

But there was only a quiet.
A final in…a final out…and then

my best friend closed his eyes
and slept.

A House Condemned

THE DEATH OF MY PEN

I've spent my life writing myself out of painful situations. I wrote myself out of a childhood where I seldom felt a mother's love. I constructed a new reality for myself back then that shielded me from the blows to my back from broom handles, extension cords, tree branches and belts wielded by the hands of a mother who never truly accepted me as her own.

I penned a protective web of protection (or so I thought) around my girly parts and my innocence even though a man called Uncle came in and stripped that web of protection away, leaving me opened wide, exposed and with no hope of closing those wounds. The wounds are still unhealed to this day.

I scribbled love songs to myself while living through a marriage in name only. A marriage whose only saving grace was my son. I suffocated most of my pain during those loveless days with booze and pain pills but it was the writing that truly brought me out of the desert of my troubled mind.

I thought those dark days were over. I thought hope and change was the new norm and finally I, too, could write poems about Nature, God, and Love. But instead, here we are, on the cusp of a new day...a day that reminds me of Jim Crow, Fallen Leaders, and 4 little girls whose brains got bashed inside a place where souls were supposed to be safe.

I'm a poet...a writer...and I'm running our of words to save myself from the pain the world is dishing out. My pen feels like it is suffocating...like it is strangling to death and all I can do is sit and watch this Code Blue situation go down.

ROOTS UNFURLED

When you look at me, you see not just an
adopted baby of unknown pedigree,

but a baby shuffled from one
Front Porch Monarch to the other,
each trying to mark me, massaging their
imprint into my skin with gnarled fingers
in an effort to make me their own.

I was a love child cradled by my daddy's callused hands.
Hands that were rubbed soft with Jergens Lotion and Vaseline
after long days of toiling for what seemed like at times
only a few dimes and nickels.

I was a country child begat by country folk
who often got pecked by the beak
of Jim Crow but who occasionally
got the chance to peck him back.

I was a blues child who jooked
just as hard as the grown folks when
J.W. Warren plucked blues harmonies
in the guise of gospel tunes in order to satisfy
both the tea drinkers and the shine sippers who
all congregated under the Saturday night altar
of stars and vast, Alabama skies.

I was a sometimes fearful child who was warned about
the Billy Bobs, Joe Nathans, and Cooter Lees
who whooped it up on back country roads and side streets—
screaming racial epithets that burned crosses into
the souls of the hearer, but in a pinch these men
would *do you right* – whether you were white or black.

But most of all
I am a storyteller who is tied to generations of other
proud storytellers whose stories
I carry in my belly like unborn babies, waiting

for the day when Emancipation comes, so I can
be one of the first to set our stories free.

A MIDWIFE'S LAMENT

Push it out Sister,
You been carrying that dead baby for way too long.
It's turning the insides of your belly
a sickly shade of green and brown.
You're all festered inside.
It's eating you up like a cancer.
Chile, ain't you ready for a fresh womb?
Ain't you ready to carry something that's gonna make you
forget them stillborn dreams and premature thoughts?
Come on, Sister.
Let me help you push it out.
You gotta know you deserve to be happy.
So come on. Let go of all that you're holding onto
and push.

COUNTRY FOLK

Country folk…indeed.

I come from southern royalty—
Sun-kissed women who stared Dixie down
and still haven't blinked.

They took words and made melodies.
Phrases rolled off their lips like Grandma's Muscadine wine.
It tasted sweet on the lips but it had a bite.

"That gal done stained her dress," Big Mama said,
eyeing one of the girls gone bad
whose belly was full of a sweat-filled night
on a back country road witha boy
everyone knew was nothing but trouble.
So now, her downfall was on everyone's tongue.
Cousin Florence shook her head in response to Big Mama's
words, "Naw Chile, that gal done ruint that dress."

They spoke in code. A click, a sigh, a moan, a string of words
that told HERstories in THEIR way—
Their names were not followed by fancy letters signifying higher
learning.

They signified with a lowness that elevated them to Queenliness.
Front Porch Matriarchs   Godheads   Rulers beyond measure
Country Folk…indeed.

HISTORY: A POEM ABOUT WATER UNDER THE BRIDGE

I peed in a Colored's Only toilet.

Where I lived, even in 1973,
Jim Crow still deemed my pee
unfit for mixed company
long after Martin had his Dream.

I was five and had to go.
We stopped at this quaint, out of the way store
but the white woman behind the counter told my Daddy,
"She can't go in here. Take her on out there."

Daddy stood tall, unblinking;
shoulders rigid and stiff,
he guided me back outside to the wooden outhouse
that was saturated with mannish-smelling piss.

He touched my shoulder
and said the only words he could,
"Hurry up now, baby girl. And don't forget to squat."

'Til this day, when peeing in public spaces,
squatting still comes more
natural than sitting.

You would think that by now I would be past this.
You would think the angry bile that used to choke
me in the middle of the night
would have subsided, abated, gone away
but the anger is still there.

Most days I can control it, suck it up and own it
But it is still there.
All these years later,
it is still there.

DARK CHILD

Dark Child, she says.
Stay out of the sun. The sun will make you black.
Look at how pretty your cousins are.
Their skin is fair. Their noses stand pert as yours lays flat.
Their hair falls in gentle waves. Your hair coils like a striking snake.
What went wrong? I never thought you'd be so black.

Mother, I say. What's wrong with me?
You're not white but your soul is bleached of color.
What's wrong with my sepia-skin?
My darkness gets blotted out by your light.
What can I do to fix what God has made?

I'm smart, Mother.
I study hard and learn big words, so you will see me.
But no words seem to validate me and you never see me.
Why don't you see me?
Can't you look at me – just once?

Dark Child, she says.
Stay out of the sun. The sun will make you black.
Look at how pretty your cousins are.
Their skin is fair. Their noses stand pert as yours lays flat.
Their hair falls in gentle waves. Your hair coils like a striking snake.
What went wrong? I never thought you'd be so black.

HUSH

Mommy, did you hear me? Uncle
    He would never do that. What did you do?
Nothing. I didn't do
    Why is your dress torn?
He ripped it. Then he made me
    Hush. Don't say that. You must have done
I didn't do anything. He grabbed me and
    I'll cook supper. You get changed and
Mommy, did you hear me? Uncle made me
    How about pizza? You like pizza. Let's order a pizza and
Mommy, did you hear me? Uncle made me touch his
    Hush. Nothing happened. Nothing happened so you should just
Hush?
    Hush.
Hush.

MOMMY ISSUES: A POEM OF DISMISSAL

Daddy and I looked for you.
Daddy looked for you in the
faces of red-lipped porcelain dolls.

I hated you
for not being those pasty-faced dolls. I ripped the ribbons they
tied to my braids, and I cursed them under my breath,
wishing it were you I assassinated with my words. I
tried to break those doll-like creatures and most times – I did.

I stopped looking for you when I found
Alice Walker. I wore my hair natural
to defy you and to embrace her. I painted my room the color purple
and retreated into the worlds that
she created.

I adopted
myself away from you and made Alice Walker my mother.
I wanted her to give birth to me in reverse.

I wanted to put all of my broken pieces
inside of Alice's womb
and, one day, in no real hurry,
I would have her push me back out again
whole and complete.

Eventually, you came back but you never returned. Daddy
tried to love you back into existence. I tried
to hate you into extinction, because see,
I didn't need you anymore. Alice Walker was my mother and
you had been dismissed.

I had read you away. Years later, I wrote you away.
I inked you out of my head. I typed you into a world
that I never had to visit, and like you,
I didn't even say goodbye.

CONSECRATED BLOOD

He treated the blood
like it was consecrated.
Didn't your mama ever tell you about the blood? he asked.

I thought of church. What can wash away my sins?
Nothing but the blood of Jesus.

But I knew this couldn't be that type of blood.

Daddy asked me again, about conversations that should have been
but he knew, never were. She'd left me in a cloud of doubt
about everything else, so it was no wonder that she had
held her lips closed – offering no balm of Gilead – about matters
such as this.

I only shook my head at him,
panic-strickened; sure that I'd somehow,
perhaps even in my dreams, sat in glass
and broke up private parts still unseen, still untouched
by the hands of any man.

All I knew was it had awakened me with a start –
brand new Cinderella sheets – wet Cinderella's face,
bloodied and battered by my restless,
sweaty, cramp-filled sleep.

Eyes opened wide upon discovering
the blood came from me. I mashed
childish hands against cotton panties stained
pink – but not girlish pink.

I had hoped with firm pressure I could stop
the flow but the blood and the belly tightening cramps
made me seek out daddy's wisdom.

I cut myself down there, I whispered. Still baby-voiced,
still unknowing of life's mysteries flowing between
my legs.

Daddy wrapped me up in gentle whispers of the secrets
that mothers should tell little girls about the changing
of their anatomy.

It was years later before I recognized
the courage it took for daddy to go out
to the little country store
and shop for just the right type of Kotex
to arm his baby girl with that morning;

the courage it took for him
to smile even though he probably wanted to cry for
his little girl who had bled and died
under the cover of Cinderella sheets.

MEMORIES: A YOUNG CHILD'S PAST-TENSE

The putrid smell of piss, stale pork rinds,
and my own vomit
linger hard in my brain.
Swallow deep, he said
and I did.
Once for the Father, Once for the Son
and Once because resistance only works
when running is an option.
And how do you run when
kneeling is the only position you know well?

"Ring around the rosy."

I used to play childish games
then I started masturbating for lack of
 a better exercise
since some dumb fuck taught
me how when I could barely walk.
He also taught me prayers and catechisms.
Go figure.

"A pocket full of posies."

Never knew sex was a game
'til I got some Judas bits of silver
to Hush-a-bye baby and not cry
then the cradle came crashing
down and broke the baby
into halves, thirds and then
into an unrecognizable mass of

"Ashes, Ashes
    We
      All
        Fall
          Down."

YEARNING FOR A SAVIOR

I waited for you.

Sought your face among the faces
of strangers, wondering if one of them
was you. But no one wanted to bundle up
my burdens and take them atop a hilltop
and die for them there.

I was plucked too soon. Vines of kudzu
suffocated my innocence leaving me
wide open, full of maggots and copperhead
venom. And still, even after all of that,
you did not try to save me.

I expected you to come with an old testament
fury and rescue me. But I grew up and
recognized savior stories as mere
Disney-like manifestations of hope
for the hopeless—fed to us like manna
from heaven and then *Poof!*
they were gone.

Perhaps it is wise you did not come.
Saviors often get crucified, and if nothing
else, the splinters of sadness that surrounded
me like wooden puddles would have left
your feet raw.

But you never came and in the end it was
I who was crucified, trying to atone for
your sins.

THESE HIPS, THESE HIPS, LORD GOD, THESE HIPS

I stand before you with these birthing Hips.
The kind of Hips that would have kept me
in a constant state of squatting, pushing out brown babies
that would have gotten stolen from me before the placenta peaked in
the middle of some night time raid from a white faced master who
wouldn't understand these Hips if Jesus Christ himself
broke it down to him in a watered down King James Version.

These Hips, these Hips, Lord God, these Hips.
They've gotten me into trouble throughout the years. My mother who
was never my mother tried to shut down the magic of
these Hips. She bound me with girdles and manifestos that said,
"Keep you and your fast-ass Hips outta these menfolk's face
or you will end up carrying a belly full of shame. Just like your REAL
mother." That woman tried to silence these Hips.
Slapped me across my mouth if I dared defend these Hips.
Told me, Satan resided in my Hips, so with that in mind,
I quieted them down to a gentle roar, but with Hips like these,
there is just so much silence they can generate.

I was called "too grown" because of these Hips. A mild-mannered nerd
girl who felt safest behind the covers of a book STILL got called out for
these Hips as I lay stretched out on MY bed. "Cover
up all them Hips," my mother would exclaim tossing a blanket at me
that felt like an oppressive winding sheet. So even in the privacy of
my own room I was taught that these Hips were dangerous. These Hips
had a life so outside of me that even in times of rest and respite I had to
watch these Hips because, hell, who knows what kind
of damage they might do without me even being aware?

I turned 11, and these Hips grew to historical proportions. I became
known as the girl with the big Hips. My Hips entered the room before
anyone noticed my face or my mind. My Hips defined me and caused
me to try and starve them into submission. I stopped eating for days
believing somehow I could nutritionally alter my Hips. But alas,
I just became a skinny assed girl with big assed Hips. They would
not go away.

It has taken years for me to make peace with these Hips. The journey started when I found out the grandmother I never knew had these Hips first. I started imagining that because she knew she would never see me up close, she would gift me these big ass Hips because she knew I would have what it takes to carry them and walk proudly into a room and dare anyone to diss me or these Hips again.

DEAR MAMA

You left me alone.
Atop tree limbs I found God.
You need not return.

A House Demolished

PHANTOM BABY

teenage sexual interlude
in back of beat-up
1963 volkswagon beetle
on a dark, alabama country road.

moon high
kudzu wrapped the ignorant
lovers in a covering
that shielded them from the view
of other ignorant lovers
seeking refuge on that same
unmarked, dirt-packed road.

sweaty bodies clumsily
attempted to affix rubber
to live man part
that still functioned
at a pre-school level
when faced with newly
grown pubic openings to his
recently crowned girlfriend who
was supposed to be for keeps.

days later, maybe weeks
but who's to say because
teenage time moves much
slower than regular time,

boy had moved on
and girl was left with the imagined
baby movements in her still flat tummy
and fantasies of little, tiny infant arms and legs
and soft baby head that would

months later be wrapped in baby blanket
that would act as a shield from the
absentee, teenage father.

but soon, bloody cramps came
and left girl grieving for
the phantom baby that never was.

she wanted that phantom baby
even though she had nothing to offer it
but her unconditional, teenage love.

THE NAKED TRUTH

I laid myself naked for you.

I exposed all of my scars – scars
as old as the Serengeti.
Tribal scars dating back before
mankind walked on two legs.

I showed you parts of me
that I was too ashamed to look at –
the underbelly;
the dark, innermost parts
that cannot be penetrated easily with the naked eye.

I trusted that you would be gentle.
I believed that you would accept
this offering of me
meant for your eyes – your eyes.

I thought you wanted to see
the folds and creases of my body without
the encumbrance of unnecessary coverings.

Were this not the case, shouldn't you have gently
blanketed me with material made of soft words
that would not have irritated the skin?

Maybe not.
Perhaps I should have just
wrapped myself from head to toe in
an emotionally-laden winding sheet of lies and deceptions.

Was I wrong about you ?
Would you rather I had covered shit up?

Maybe that's it – maybe I should go back to wearing
layers of clandestine emotions sewn together with
threads of half-truths and misnomers.

I get it now.

Today I'll go shopping and buy a new wardrobe
that will effectively make my outside
look aesthetically pleasing to the eye
so that you don't have to be
offended by the sight of my shit *lain bare*.

FRIGID

cold-natured.
hard to thaw.
ice water in your veins.

all monikers he placed on me.

but

it was   his touch   that started winter storms to form in my soul.
it was   his kiss   that turned my lips frostbite blue.

it was   his jack frost like nature   that caused the cold breath
to seep from my dry, moist-free lips.

he   was supposed to be   the thermal blanket
wrapped   tightly around   shoulders and arms needing heat.

he   was supposed to   shield me, melt me, warm me   through the
night.

he   was supposed to be   the spring   bringing thaw
to my winter-weary mind   frozen hard
by years of blizzard conditions   and   black ice moments.

he   was supposed to   melt the winter snow   accumulations   thick
inside   my heart breaking   ice   barriers down   so

i   would   be   cold
                              no more.

SORRY?

I'm sorry you're addicted to
watered down, soulless creatures
who don't speak the truth.

It saddens me that at full strength
I am sometimes hard for you to digest.

I get it, I am a mouthful.
I don't go down easy.
I can spew venom that can
upset your stomach.

You'd like me better if I were
more like the liquid diet they
assign to you when you are too weak-stomached
to hold solid foods.

I hate that for you,
because you are missing out.
Yes, I can be like a dish over-spiced
with cayenne pepper sometimes, but I can also
tease your palate like a dark espresso, triple latte
with just a hint of cream.

But you have to be prepared to take all of this in,
and digest all parts of me because it is too late
in my life for me to mess around and try and change
the recipe.

Do what you must do to take me in.
Just know that asking me to stop being me
is no longer an option.

BITCH

Sometimes I bark and growl and
snarl and bare my teeth.

I pull hard on the chains
you have tied me down with
in order to domesticate me.

I spread my legs
and give birth to these – my progeny
that you will not even come out
of your house to see.

Helpless I am to their pitiful yelps.
They are cold;
defenseless;
unloved.

So what am I left to do?

Kill my young rather
than see those restless pups
left for dead by you?

No, I keep them close to me;
nipping at them,
slapping them with my paw,
doing all the things that I can do
to keep them from becoming wild, uncontrollable
beasts.

Day by day
I pace the yard from side to side –
anxious for a time when you forget
to lock the gate

So that we can run away – free.

VACATION

Sometimes I checked out.
I would literally sign the tab,
say thank you for the room,
and then I would leave.

I'd rush past the bellman
crashing out of the hotel room
 running blindly towards the lobby
dragging behind me luggage crammed with dark secrets
and hidden shames.

And I wasn't checking out to go to a better place.
I went on no extended vacations to exotic locations. I
retreated to back wooded areas—places undiscovered
by human eyes. I built shelter out of kudzu.

I unpacked my luggage and draped myself
in all of the pain it contained. Then I waited
giving the kudzu time to wrap itself around
me until I was a mummified mess. Until
I was so far gone that the screams of my son
sounded like whispers. He'd yell: *Mommy where are you?*

I wanted to answer but I didn't know how. There
were no maps to where I was and even if
there were, I didn't want him to come and
see me there. So at times I'd manage to weakly call
back to him: *Don't worry. Mommy will be back.*

I made it seem like we were playing an elaborate game
of hide and seek. I made him believe that Mommy's
condition was normal or that it was Halloween and I
was in disguise. *Shhhh. Let's be quiet and the
Voices won't be able to find us.* He'd play the
game until he'd get tired. *Mommy come back.*

And for him, I would drag myself back.
I'd repack the sadness the bitterness and the shame
back into the suitcases and then I'd unravel the
ropes of kudzu that clung to me like an Anaconda ready to
suck my very life away. Tired and exhausted
I would gather my boy in my arms. *It's okay*, I'd say.
I'm back. Mommy is back.

I MUST NOT BREATHE

If I am stopped by the cops I must be quiet.
I must not breathe.
I must not ask questions.
I must not breathe.
I must not move.
I must not breathe.
I must not talk back.
I must be compliant.
I must not breathe.
I must not film the cop.
I must not call family or friends.
I must not breathe.
I must not put my hands up or down.
I must not breathe.
I must cooperate.
I must be docile.
I must stay in the car or get out, depending on the mood of the cop.

I must not breathe too loudly or too quietly.
I must only do what I am told even if what I am told to do goes against
my basic civil rights.
I must not breathe.
I must hope that the cop is having a good day.
I must hope that the cop is a "good cop."
I must hold my breath and not breathe.
I must not be suicidal.
I must not be angry.
I must be civil.
I must be obedient.
I must grin and show all of my teeth.
I must shuffle and dance, but only on cue.
I must not get stopped but if I run, I must be prepared to die.
I must be prepared to die.
I must be prepared to die, even on a routine stop.
I must not breathe.
I must not breathe.
I must not breathe.

I'M TIRED OF LIVING IN A WORLD

I'm tired of living in a world where penises
are granted more power than vaginas.
A world where testosterone is the fuel that
propels leaders into positions where they treat
women like poor missionaries without a voice
or a claim to the lands they inhabit.

I'm tired of wondering if our daughters and granddaughters
will ever be allowed to speak for their body parts
or will they continue to be turned into mini-Barbies
whose only function is to be window-dressers
for department stores run by Dicks and no Janes.

Must we always live in a world where we can't
speak up for the anatomically incorrect
dolls who are supposed to represent the ideal feminine form
but in whose mind I wonder? Is there a benevolent god
who's in charge of this miserable mess or maybe God is
a goddess who actually believes an apple and a snake
was enough to render us voiceless for generation after
generation – but either way, be it God or Goddess, I say

it is time for women to reclaim our anatomy and our minds.
It is time for women to say out loud that we will not stop
Until justice truly rolls down like waters that drown
The patriarchal, dictatorial voices forever.

A House Salvaged

DRY BONES

Like dry bones in the valley
you left me for dead,

but I was my own Ezekiel.
I asked myself,
Can these bones live?

I didn't know the answer,
but I called to them.
I knew if I didn't order those bones to live
no one else would.

I knew that death had whispered my name
and it was up to me to scream louder
and take away its sting and
to reclaim those bones and demand them
to rise up again.

I called each and every bone by name.
I called flesh to those bones
and then I cried out to the four winds
so that breath would enter that body again.

And the winds answered back   my body was made new,
and I was no longer cut off from that
which was rightly mine.

I stood up with a great and mighty shout.
Ready to do battle.
Ready to claim that which was mine.
Ready to live in these bones again.

BLACK GIRL MAGIC

We're not magic because we're black or girls.

We're magic, because years ago, back when slave catchers
came and tried to steal our magic away,
we still held on to enough of that shit to
protect our progeny from extinction.

Stripped, lain bare, ripped wide open like
 a slaughtered lamb, all of our magic
began to seep from our pores, drizzle down our legs and fertilize this
earth so others could reap a harvest born from
our leftover magical residue.

Hell yeah, we black girls got magic. And we know
that shit scares some of you. That's why you try to tame us, silence
us, corner us into a small portion of the room
with the belief that our magic will go away. But hell naw.
That marvelous magic is too old to go away. It can be found in
the tombs of the ancient Kings and Queens, and if you aren't careful
those dry bones will rise up and walk the earth again.

Oh yeah, some tried to trick us with their mind games.
Told us our magic was evil and dark but then stole
it for their own pleasure and our pain. Defiance
was the first of our magic that was stolen.
Then came pride. Next came love of self, but one
bit of magic that could not be stolen was hope.

We had boat loads of that magic. Enough to damn
near cause the slave catchers boats to float upside down. We had
those boats rocking with our power as we
floated in a cesspool of lies
misconceptions and half truths

We did not stop though. We held on to that old magic and
we let it spring from our breasts into the mouths
of our young. We fed those babies hope when we
had nothing else to nourish their little bodies with.

We cloaked ourselves with Hope when we were sold away
from everything we knew and loved. We stooped down
low and picked up the dirt that held the footprint of the
last step of our loved ones as they got drug away from us.

We swallowed that dirty hope
believing it would one day reunite us with all that we had
lost and loved.

Now, fast forward to the present time. We are still taking
large bites of that hope and impregnating ourselves
with it. We are making magic for all the world to see.
So, call it black girl magic. Call it ancestral spirits rising
up. Call it whatever you want, but just know this, you can't
ever take it from us. No matter how hard you might try.

I TRIED TO WRITE YOU A LOVE POEM
BUT THEN IT BECAME ABOUT ME

One day, I woke up
and I felt something stirring,
something inside of me was quivering.
I mean, it was like some righteous heat
swelling up inside of me.

It was burning like volcano-mountain-top burning;
like Moses and the burning bush burning;
like fire baptized burning;
generating enough heat
that I almost had to
Stop.

And take a breath.

I was like, damn, what was that?
I looked over at who would soon become my ex
and thought to myself that even on a good day,
he never made me feel like that.

I kicked his ass out straightway.
That day.
I claimed the power inside of me.
I was like, if I can generate all that heat,
in my sleep,
what the hell do I need him for?
So I threw his shit out the door.
Then, I went on a quest to discover
what else I could do.
Alone.
By myself.
Without the aiding and abetting of anyone else.

I discovered I could fly.
I discovered I could stretch out my arms like wings
And literally soar to another plain.

I even had the audacity to think that
even in my saddest moments,
if I tried, I could cry and turn my tears into rain.

I imagined I had thunderstorms brewing in these thighs
and mountains forming from these hips.
I even thought my ass caused suns to set and noonday solar eclipses.

Once I discovered that I am good, hell, great
and that with or without a man
I'm straight –

That's when I became set free
to open up my heart, my soul, and my mind
And accept you. Welcome You.
Because I didn't need to be made complete.
I was whole and the only thing I needed you to do for me
was to just be.

HAVING A LOVE AFFAIR WITH MY DAMN SELF

I came looking for an old friend today called Me.
I said, "Hey girl, what's up?"
I tried to look away
but I touched my face
and made me look…made me look at…made me look at me.

I said, "Girl, you are looking fine."
I trembled under the heat of the audacity of my own stare.
I took my hand and said, "Get dressed, we're going out."
And we did.

We had some drinks, got up and swayed
to some Marvin Gaye. I rolled my hips
keeping time to the beat. I held me close, closed my eyes
and felt my own heat start to rise.

That's when we left.

I took me home,
drank more wine
Then I said, "Yo Ma, you gonna give me a peak
at your honey sweet?"
And you know what? I did.

I stripped me down
loved on every scar, every mark, every part of me
I'd deemed a flaw. Loved me back
into existence like only I could do.

I touched myself in places I had
ignored, covered up in shame, or
decided was too imperfect for even my own eyes
to see. I loved me forward and back again.

I said, "Damn, you're beautiful!"
"Damn, you're a Queen."
"Damn, you're Nomvula—that mean's 'after the rain.'"
That means you are a lifebringer, Ma.

You are sunshine, you are moonbeams, you are
 earth, you are stars, you are galaxies, you
are universes undiscovered, you are nebulas,
you are all that and more.

Girl, say your own damn name.

And I did. I screamed my name to the heavens
and the heavens screamed back.

I fed myself large portions of me
and I was full. So right then I knew for sure that
if I was a prayer there would be nothing left to say but
Amen.

BLUES HIGH

Your music
makes me want
to strip down, fling my
naked body onto
each riff
each bend
each slide

until I'm blue black
with ink from
every musical note
you've written
inside your mind.

Write a song about me
and play
it on that guitar;

that guitar
you're strumming
on right now.

Make
that guitar
cry out my name.

Strum me into
a sexfunkyfrenzy.

Grunt out some harmonies like
MuddyWatersHowlin'WolfTampaRedJohnLeeHookerAndBuddyGuy.

Put down some serious pulsating rhythms along my neck
towards my back
down my arms
over my stomach
and between my thighs.

Come on, play me something hotsexyfast

because tonight, I wanna be
blues high.

I AM NOT YOUR CORPORATE MAMMY

I am not your Corporate Mammy.

I will offer you no tit filled with
Compassion's milk so that you can deal with me.

I will not belittle my mind by babysitting your fragile ego
as day after day it comes into play.

I will not be carted out as your Number 1 token Negro so
you can look diversified while my soul
slowly dies inside.

I will not revamp my attitude so your fear
of my power will go away.

I will not attend your meetings and speak articulately, so that I can
be the spokesperson for the entire black race.

I unapologetically refuse to give birth
to any more ideas that you feel free to steal away and sell
as if it were from your loins they sprang.

I will not straighten or tame down my hair
because depending on my mood, I look
militant to you.

I will not grin and smile in your face when all I want
is to be left alone so I can regroup
and get ready to face another day.

I am not your Corporate Mammy.
There I said it, put it out there, and I will not take
it back, retract, or try to say this in a more pleasant way.

So my advice to you, is as long as your work gets done,
timely and in a professional way,
back up and give a Sista some room,
Or you will get a taste
of some sho nuff, straight from the country
Black Rage.

PLAY ME ONE OF THOSE OLD SCHOOL JOINTS: AND I'LL BE YOURS TONIGHT

Baby, you know me.

Music
gets me high. And when
you sing and play for me,
just for me,

for a moment
for a solitary moment

it's. like. I. can. fly.

You let loose with one of those
old school joints
And I can't think straight.

And when you strum that guitar –

When you strum that guitar just right
making melodies hard, fast and divine –

Well, when you do all that –
Baby, when you do all that
there ain't no doubt,

I am yours tonight.

BACCHUS, ARE YOU THERE?

Hello, Bacchus.
Is that you lurking in my mind?

I'm sitting on the porch
sipping Muscadine wine made
by withered, hands the color of burnt wood.

Sipping it slowly,
I knew you'd probably slither
inside of my mind because you're Bacchus
and that is what you do.

You know what I'm doing?
I'm trying to escape
from these rural thoughts
that strangle me like
a hang man's noose.

There's me – high in a tree
my legs flopping in the wind
like a scarecrow – devoid of life –
devoid of soul.

I am strange fruit.

I'm also a southern girl
born in the sanctified south
where there is only supposed to be
one God and one Way, so, I ask you,
how did you find me
or, did I go looking for you?

You're not welcome here, Bacchus. These
saints filled with holy ghosts that make
them flit and flail about would not
understand godheads who ruled before

Christ took his first step
or turned water into wine.

They will drive you away
or water you down Disney-style
so that you don't scare them
with your power to reveal
the raw underbelly of a person's soul.

I don't fear you, Bacchus.
I welcome you with open arms.

I am a bottomless vessel
ready to be filled with the old wine
that you have to offer that will
render me prostrate on the floor
as I wait to receive your kiss – chaste
but intoxicating.

Come for me, Bacchus.

At any moment
I expect to see you ride up
on a leopard and spirit me away
for good. I'll go with you.

Will you sew me up in your thigh
like Zeus did for you in your infancy?
I need shielding too. If you put me
there I will willingly
go with you – I will let my madness go
because it is a shield that I will no longer need.

Funny how you fit so well
in my southern world of pine trees
and magnolia blooms and
front porch gods and goddesses
who sit
spinning tales of long-gone

giants who made us
feel like we too were descendants
of gods.

I hate that they don't remember you.

Bacchus
if that is you, and I believe that it is,
come and get me now. Don't worry,
I'll go with you and I will leave
my madness at home.

NAKED COMMUNION

Nude.
I want my naked body to be
free again.

Free of inhibition;
free of any fears I might have of reprisal;
free of embarrassment at allowing my breasts, my hips and my thighs
to languish without restrictive binding in the hot, summer sunlight.

I want to
bake myself back to the royal shade
of black that once kissed my skin
in another lifetime
before I had to worry about hair being good
and skin being light.

I want to roll back and forth
in the mud by an Alabama creek bottom
near the spot where I grew up
and cover myself with that mud
until I look tribal;
until my inner warrior cries out
like a Zulu Priestess who has been
held hostage in a foreign land for way too long.

I want my tongue to taste that dirt.
I want to pack it inside my mouth
until I can taste the historical past, present and future
in that dirt. I want to swallow it until my ancestors' souls
begin to take root in my stomach –
a stomach that bursts forth with trees
whose names are foreign but whose branches and leaves
gather me up in an embrace of familiarity.

Then,
I want to dance naked in the rain.
I want to let my head fall back as I open my mouth and let

Heaven's teardrops bathe me, caress me, drown me
and wash me clean so that I can start

the process all over again. Naked and free.

52

I BELONG TO PAN

The god Pan overtakes me in a scarily
erotic
Dance.

Erect, always at attention,
He caters to my every desire –
both known and unknown.

I know not where these
feelings stem from
that he generates from me
each time he touches me
or follows my movement
with long glances. When he stares
it is always
my eyes that look
away first.

This lust – this passion
bubbles up inside of me
like volcanic overflow.
I crave his godhead to enter
me and wear me down
until I lie in a whimpering
mass at Pan's feet.

I want
To be his concubine;
his whore,
his wench.

Don't judge me.
If you had known Pan, like I have known Pan
you, too,
would willingly lie underneath
the weight of his manhood

without fear of reprisal
or sadness in the unexpected disappearance
of your 60's inspired, bra-burning,
Gloria Steinem ways.

54

YOU BLACK

You black.
You blue black.
You boot black.
You straight up soot black.
You African, some tribe I can't pronounce black.
You tar on the highway black.
You Crayola crayon in the box black.
You coal, straight outta some mining shaft black.
You Color Purple Shug Avery saying "You so ugly" black.
You blacker than black black.
You black, so black I can't see you at night black.
You bona fide, certified, straight up out of the country black.
You black cat take away all the good juju black.

But is that really black?

Isn't black, Motherland, home of where civilization started black?
Isn't black, rain clouds bringing life back to all living things black?
Isn't black, Jesus Christ, hair like lamb's wool black?
Isn't black, brought us over on slave ships but all these years later we
still standing black?
Isn't black, hunted down with dogs and strung up on trees but we
still got through it together black?
Isn't black, Rosa Parks "ain't gonna sit in the back of the bus no more"
black?
Isn't black, King saying "I have a Dream" and we believed it black?
Isn't black, 70's black power, black-gloved throw up your fist and
pump it black?

Isn't black, dreadlocks, airfros, cornrows and fades black?
Isn't black, Parliaments "Make my funk the P.Funk, I wants to get
funked up" black?
Isn't black, Michael doing the moonwalk for the first time on television
black?
Isn't black, underground hip hop before it got hijacked by the masses
black?
Isn't black, Shirley Chisolm, Jesse Jackson, Al Sharpton, and Barack
Obama making history black?

I say we've got to redefine black. We've got to go out and be explorers and unearth the truth about black, so we can rediscover what black used to be and what it can be again. We got to take black back from the thieves and robbers who stole its essence and its beauty so they know it ain't that damn easy to wipe out black.

So, are you with me? Are you ready to go on a journey with me to reclaim black back?

WE CUT

We cut our hair.
Three generations of lambs who sheered our own woolly locs.

It was our new beginning.
We weren't lambs going to slaughter;
we were self-appointed shepherds who herded ourselves
out of bad conditions into new beginnings and it started
with our hair.

We cut away layers of shame,
lengths of hurt.
We ripped out matted clumps of hairy suggestions
that we weren't good enough.

Cutting left our heads free of the past and
the stubble left promise of new growth.

Three generations
separated by miles, no knowledge of the others' fleecing,
no knowledge that our individual strengths represented generational
courage
born probably from generations of women who knew
that their strength was in the cutting.

We were not
that one sheep that made the shepherd leave the ninety-nine.
We knew we must shepherd ourselves into our own new beginnings
if we did not want to remain lost.

We were a herd made up of three generations of
full grown sheep – separated by distance but
united by the cutting of hair.

A House Rebuilt

KARMA

It always
all
comes back
to you.

Sew those
impossible
untraceable seeds
of discord
in unfertile
land
and you will
still reap
a bountiful
crop of karma
blossoms
that burst forth
into strange fruit
that will
inevitably
taste just like
you.

REBIRTH

I think I loved him because
he said that time – that other time
didn't count.

He said
it was blotted out of the collective memory – his and mine
like sins washed clean by Jesus' blood.

He said
we'd never mention it again.
He said it would be like it never happened,
and my virginity would be restored to me and
like a newly, baptized saint – I would be made new.

So naturally, without even thinking,
I let him pluck the cherries from this – my
newly reblossomed tree. Never once
thinking that maybe he, too, would chop
me down, leaving me in splinters.

AN ODE TO MY REBELLIOUS SON

You began your life wanting to come out.
From day one, you rebelled against the marginalization
of a nine month commitment.

You said, I will not arrive this date or that.
I will show up when it feels right to me.
I both feared and celebrated your nonconformity.

You were feisty – before you even knew the difference between
an arabesque and a pas de basque
you were a mover – I knew a dancer's spirit lived in my belly.

On the day you finally said enough to confinement,
you further showed your disdain for the establishment
and began your adventure by showing the world your ass first.

Painful though it was for me to have them try and turn you,
there was a small satisfaction in me
when it became clear that you would not be moved.

When they pealed my belly back for you to make your grand entrance
I couldn't help but smile at you through my pain.
I finally felt that connection to you

as your little fist pumped in the air as if to say
Hello world, I'm here, but on my terms
I knew I'd met my love, my true love – my rebellious son.

SPIRIT WOMAN

I am Spirit-Woman. I flit
and flee
and follow a path that is
unseen to the
naked eye.

I glide through time
and space leaving
no traceable path
for you to follow
so that you can find
me once I'm gone.

I never really leave
but I do go to other
realms of existence
that, like a great gulf
separates me from you.

I am Spirit-Woman.
I am wind-storms.
I am comets blazing
across dark night skies.
I am hurricanes that
won't get pinned down
by man-made names
or machines that try to track
my path.

I am uncontrollable
heat on a summer day
that crushes indexes
told by suit-clad
weathermen who don't have
a clue
that I cannot be studied
or understood.

I am life.

WHERE THE MUSIC AT?

Hey ma – why you all the time sounding so angry?

Don't you have some rhymes about
when a man fingered you up,
getting you all saxed up,
making you cry out jazz notes
to the tune of the *yardbird*
scratch, scratch, scratching your blues away?

I swear to god, one man treat you bad and you
can't hear the music no more –
one man treat you bad and
you give him the power to play the rhythm
clean out your soul.

You need to ride the *trane*, girl,
and let some *miles* get between you
and him or whoever took your music away.

You need to let them evil thoughts
spin up out of your mind
and get you *dizzy* over *gillespie*
so you can bebop your way back home again.

You need to let your mind
be free so you can hear
rashied ali thumping
your drums, ma
bump twa, bump twa, bump twa.

How you gonna let the rhythm reverberate
through your hips again
if you don't let that earthy beat
call out your name?

Put on some *hendrix*
and let some disharmonies
roll you back into a *thelonious* mood.

Come on, baby.
Write something with a hook
but with no words and
scat yourself back into a happy mood
doo-ah, doo-ah, doo-ah.

Rhyme us something, baby, just me and you,
that's gonna make us both feel good tonight.

LOCS
To my husband, Robert

I feel his hands reaching into the thick wild kudzu that is my hair.

His fingers dig deep
pulling hair from its hiding places against my scalp,
using ancient herbs and oils to seduce my hair
to grudgingly accept his plea to lock.

Who would think such pale fingers
would understand the mysteries
of this kinky universe that sprouted from my head
even better than me,

but he approaches it with a familiarity;
negotiating with it
reasoning with its resistance to conformity.

He seems to understand that
it wants to define its own pattern;
it wants to climb and explore with the freedom of kudzu –
uninhibited, untamed, unmanaged.

Locking feels confining to this wild mane that
wants nothing more than to move itself freely
around my ears
across my eyes into my nostrils
into and out through my mouth
so that it can lace tightly around my tongue
bringing silence to a tongue
that might not get its story right.

Rebellious and demanding hair that it is,
it commandeers acknowledgment from all. It says: I am jaTaa.
I am Rasta. I am Jew. I am Hindu. I am Islam. I am Christian.
I am ancient. It says bow down to me.

He, with the reverent fingers, steeped with respect,
validates these locs through his submission to them.

He gently coaxes out the spirits of the ancestors
who live in this sovereign land of coiled twists.

Afterwards, when he is done communing with my hair,
I look at myself with a newness, appreciating
this crown that adorns my head.

I can finally see the ancestors in me for the first time
and they, likewise, can finally see me, and they,
with smiles of recognition,
acknowledge and welcome me home.

HOUSE REPAIRS

What you stole from me
wasn't yours.

I didn't offer it,
you took it.
You broke in and
ransacked every room;
tore down load-bearing walls and
crashed through doors that were closed shut;
smashed windows leaving broken, jagged glass.

But I'm rebuilding.
Stronger.
Better.
Newer.

You didn't win.
I'm still here.
This house is still here.

ANGELA JACKSON-BROWN

Angela Jackson-Brown is an award-winning writer, poet and playwright who teaches Creative Writing and English at Ball State University in Muncie, IN. She is a graduate of the Spalding low-residency MFA program in Creative Writing. She is the author of the novel *Drinking From A Bitter Cup* and has published in numerous literary journals. Recently Angela's play, *Anna's Wings,* was selected to be a part of the IndyFringe DivaFest her play *Flossie Bailey Takes a Stand* was part of the Indiana Bicentennial Celebration at the Indiana Repertory Theatre. She also wrote and produced the play *It Is Well* and she was the co-playwright with Ashya Thomas on a play called B*lack Lives Matter (Too).* In the spring of 2018, Angela co-wrote a musical with her colleague, Peter Davis, called *Dear Bobby: The Musical,* that was part of the 2018 OnxyFest in Indianapolis, IN. *House Repairs* will be her first published book of poetry.

CPSIA information can be obtained
at www.ICGtesting.com
Printed in the USA
LVHW021613141021
700428LV00006B/690